MY TEACHER
Remembering Marcel Moyse

Susan S. Fries

with illustrations by Erik Wong

Bloomington, IN  Milton Keynes, UK

authorHOUSE®

AuthorHouse™
1663 Liberty Drive, Suite 200
Bloomington, IN 47403
www.authorhouse.com
Phone: 1-800-839-8640

AuthorHouse™ UK Ltd.
500 Avebury Boulevard
Central Milton Keynes, MK9 2BE
www.authorhouse.co.uk
Phone: 08001974150

First published by AuthorHouse 5/8/2007

ISBN: 978-1-4259-8908-8 (hc)
ISBN: 978-1-4259-8909-5 (sc)

Library of Congress Control Number: 2007900357

Printed in the United States of America
Bloomington, Indiana

This book is printed on acid-free paper.

Cover Design by Mark Divers

MARCEL MOYSE

May 17, 1889: Born, St. Amour, France.

Student of Hennebains, Gaubert and Taffanel.

1905: Age 16, he graduated (receiving First Prize) from Paris Conservatory.

1913: US Tour with soprano, Nellie Melba, opening a new era for solo flute performances.

First flutist in the most important French orchestras, including Paris Opera and Opera-Comique. Conductors played under include Richard Strauss, Bruno Walter, Furtwangler, Toscanini and Prokofieff.

1920's, 30's and 40's: He was the most recorded of all French flutists. Last recordings produced privately in 1954: *The French School at Home,* and *Tone Development Through Interpretation.*

The Moyse Trio toured Europe and South America.

1932-1940: Professor of Flute at Paris Conservatory.

1932: Performed J.S. Bach *Brandenburg Concerto No. 5* with Suisse Romande Orchestra, Ernest Ansermet, conductor.

1934: Premier performance in Prague of Jacques Ibert *Concerto* written for him. Roussel dedicated first movement of his *Joneurs de Flute* to him.

1951: First summer of performances at Marlboro Festival, founded by Marcel Moyse, Rudolph Serkin and Adolf Busch. Marlboro recordings include *Octet, Opus 103 for Winds,* conducted by Moyse, among others.

1964-1983: Flute and Wind (oboe, clarinet, French horn and bassoon) seminars in Switzerland, Marlboro, St.Amour, London, Tokyo, Matsumoto, Kobe and Los Angeles. Famous flute students included Aurele Nicolet, Raymond Meylan, James Galway, Robert Aitken, Paula Robison.

Throughout his lifetime: Moyse authored/composed many publications and methods, 37 books of etudes covering all aspects of traditional flute playing. His beautiful art adorns several of his book covers and his hand manuscript is contained in some.

November 1, 1984: Died at home in Brattleboro, Vermont. Buried in St. Amour, France.

Remembering Marcel Moyse

To: Lydia Sarandan, for her inspiration, in the middle of a parking lot, after I told her a funny story from my teacher, Marcel Moyse.

To: Liz Goldner, who asked endless questions that forced me to clarify and simplify so that she as a non-musician could understand every word.

To: Laura, my beautiful daughter and wise advisor, who beyond her magnificent vocal talent, has an amazing ability to change a thought into a dynamic phrase.

TABLE OF CONTENTS

"The most beautiful thing we can experience is the mysterious. It is the source of all true art and science."

Albert Einstein

PRELUDE

I

I first met Marcel Moyse in 1967 when he came to Oberlin Conservatory, Ohio to conduct special master classes for the centennial celebration there.

We connected almost immediately, and I subsequently spent time with Moyse as a student, as a host and as a friend. I often visited his home in Brattleboro, Vermont for lessons and seminars. In January 1981, he stayed at my home in Newport Beach, traveling daily to Los Angeles to give special flute and woodwind classes to qualified musicians. The 15 years I knew him were a long series of wonderful, enlightening adventures.

As a master teacher, Moyse expressed a joyous and adventurous spirit, a love of life and an infectious sense of humor. He was passionate, possessing a deep sensitivity to everything in life from nature, to the physical environment, to people.

He did not have an easy life. After a celebratory musical start, his path was interrupted over and over again by fragile health and by the overwhelming effects of the German occupations in France during the two world wars. Because of his struggles, Moyse had an incredible will to live, to make music and to inspire all musicians. He was devoted to his family and to his music.

Moyse continues to have a profound effect on me as a musician and as a person, as well as on all those who worked with him or know him through his many published materials.

There was a sweetness about him, along with a devilish twist. His charming manner often contrasted with his feistiness; he occasionally exploded into brief tirades when an interviewer, biographer, colleague or student failed to understand him or the music they were playing.

Marcel Moyse brought out genius in students, even when they did not know that this quality existed within them. His techniques of teaching were legendary, sometimes theatrical and always charming. In order to convey the character of a piece of music, or even a certain phrase, Moyse often narrated a colorful story from his own life or used analogies from the physical world. (For example, "Reach for the stars," or "the bouncing ball.") Woodwind players, who heard the music within his message, learned how to dynamically bring composers' music to life.

As Moyse's magnificent reputation preceded my initial meeting with him, I put myself totally in his hands. From our first meeting, I recorded many of his lessons, seminars, stories and jokes. Today, I have 100 hours of these recordings, plus copious notes and signs written on my music. I treasure all of this material—much of which provides background for this book.

It is nearly 25 years since I last saw my teacher. Yet, I continually hear his voice and often hear myself saying his words when I work with my own flute and chamber music students. Moyse said that he heard his own teacher, Taffanel, who in turn heard his teacher, who belonged to a legacy that stretches far back into the past.

This book is a collection of my personal and professional experiences with Marcel Moyse. (A well-written biography by Ann McCutchen, *Marcel Moyse, The Voice of the Flute*, contains more descriptions with significant dates, places and people in and around his life, as well as a complete list of publications and discography of Marcel Moyse, available from Amadeus Press, Portland, Oregon.)

Moyse is my guardian angel. For this, I am grateful beyond words! It is my deepest desire that while reading this book, you will wish you had known this man.

II

Marcel Moyse was born May 17, 1889 in St. Amour, France, during a period when French Impressionism was flourishing and influencing artistic movements worldwide. As a young man in the early 20th century, Marcel excelled in painting as well as in music. But his love for the flute – his astonishingly beautiful tone and musicianship – attracted musical opportunities, which saved him from the impoverished lifestyle, common to many painters in Paris. However, he continued to think like a painter, using music and tone as his oils and watercolors.

At age 21, Moyse fell in love with Celine Gautreau, a beautiful dancer who performed at the Gaité Lyric Theatre. He married her in 1912, and considered her to be the greatest benefit of his life. Celine in turn was devoted as a wife and mother of two, and became indispensable to Marcel's health. Moyse, always a strong family man, often said, "I am nothing without my family."

Although musicians must perform in major cities, he was happiest in his country childhood home of St. Amour. Nearly every August, he returned there for an entire month. In that rejuvenating pastoral setting, he indulged in his lifelong love of painting, spending numerous hours outdoors, recording the country landscape. He loved the "naturelle."

Mr. Moyse was very prone to asthmatic and pneumatic conditions, which resulted in his disqualification as a soldier in World Wars I and II. During the First World War, Moyse's family rented a small Paris apartment, escaping the war from time to time in St. Amour. Very little musical work was available—Moyse had to reduce by half his price for lessons and take any engagement he could. The family experienced hunger, sometimes for days. At the end of the war, Mr. Moyse could not play the flute—his pneumonia was so serious. At that time, he resolved to, "fight for life or die!"

After World War I, he was appointed first flutist at the Opera Comique and spent his summers resting and restoring his soul in St. Amour. The summers gave him time to paint, walk, drive around the countryside, as well as play billiards, drink Pernod and smoke his pipe while he daydreamed. In 1931, he was appointed Professor of Flute at Paris Conservatory. This position ended with the German invasion of Paris in 1940.

During World War II, Moyse was again disappointed that he could not serve France; he continued to harbor bitterness toward the Nazis. To confound his frustration, they arrested and humiliated him in Paris, as the name "Moyse" had a Jewish connotation. But because he was Catholic, they released him.

After a long, fearful, musically barren (except for his prodigious writings) and isolating time in occupied France, Moyse returned to Paris Conservatory to reinstate his professorship. Unfortunately, the school did not wait for his return and a replacement had been hired. He fought like a tiger to get his position back, only obtaining a secondary flute class. But his pride won out and he quit [spewing some well-chosen expletives, including 'merde'] as soon as he won the position.

The disillusioned Moyse family packed up and sailed to Argentina to hopefully avail themselves of opportunities to perform and teach there, along with other famous displaced musicians from Europe. Simultaneously, Argentinean President Juan Peron took office and closed universities and concert venues, forcing many transplanted European musicians to leave the country.

Rudolph Serkin, long established in America as a pianist, suggested to the Moyse family that they immigrate to the United States—to live near Marlboro, Vermont and to teach at Marlboro College as The Moyse Trio. They could settle in countryside that was very much like their motherland. In 1949, they gratefully immigrated to the US and stayed for good. (Please see Part One, "The Founding of Marlboro Music Festival," for more information.)

Moyse's reputation preceded him, and participants in his Vermont flute seminars came from the United States, Canada, England, Australia, Japan and Switzerland. Many stayed in small local hotels and private homes in surrounding towns for 10-day periods. Some individuals took apartments in town to study for as long as possible.

At some seminars, Moyse's students were acutely aware of his courageous struggles to breathe. At one distressing class, the attendees were on edge, waiting for a spasm to end and the next breath to finally come. However, he never made excuses for his condition and gracefully continued to teach. His powerful underlying message is that the spirit and will—not the obstacles—control the artist. In fact, he emanated exuberance, no matter what his physical or emotional condition.

Moyse's hands were supple when I knew him, with no signs of arthritis or distortion, other than slenderness from old age. He claimed that playing the flute is the ideal exercise for the hands; as they are elevated, the flute weighs very little, and the technique is light.

In many instances where Moyse's command of English was inadequate, he communicated through his animated face and eyes, as well as through body language – sometimes dancing and singing. Inspired by the gestures of the famous mime artist, Marcel Marceau (b. 1923), Moyse skillfully used pantomime to reveal characters in the music.

As a man of great integrity, Monsieur Moyse was adamant about his dislike for a famous oboist compatriot from Paris Conservatory, Marcel Tabuteau. Truly a giant performer—later known as a cleverly mean but fantastic teacher—Moyse believed that the oboist had "bad character."

He often told the following story about Tabuteau. "He bragged that during World War I, he had switched his un-cleaned gun with that of the soldier standing next to him. Shortly afterward, the poor soldier was killed in battle, perhaps because his gun would not shoot properly." Moyse pointed out, "Character flaws don't disappear just because someone has been called to be an artist." Hitler was reputed to be a good painter!

Moyse's favorite violinist was Fritz Kreisler. His favorite pianist was Jacques Thibeau. He remarked that Enrico Caruso had a beautiful voice, saying, "Everything was in the right place," meaning that his singing was true to the musical score. "On his second phrase, he elongated the important high note, developing the beauty of his voice, breathing before it so he could develop more."

Mr. Moyse had a keen awareness of the progression of the many musical masters who came before him, understanding that each inspired those who followed. However, he had the wisdom to know his value and place in tradition, and especially the humility that never allowed him to call himself "Master." (Many students lovingly referred to him as 'Le Maitre.')

"My candle was lit in me;
I light a candle in the next ones."
Marcel Moyse

"I am obliged to pass on the honored tradition
of the French School whatever that is!"
Marcel Moyse

PART ONE – OBERLIN MASTER CLASSES (DECEMBER 1967)

HOW WE MET

HOW HE WORKED

HE INVITED HIMSELF FOR LUNCH

MY FOUR-HOUR LESSON

Sometimes the people we meet
change us forever.

HOW WE MET

I first met Marcel Moyse, the famous French master of the flute, when he came to Oberlin Conservatory, Ohio in 1967 to conduct special master classes for their centennial celebration. I was a faculty member, mother of three small children and wife of a highly respected French horn player/professor.

When I first set eyes on the 78-year-old Marcel Moyse, he looked to me like a French Impressionist painter. He wore a colorful ascot around his neck, a light cotton batiste shirt in tiny black and white checks, layering a heavier green shirt and an overcoat for warmth. He had a handkerchief in his shirt pocket, which was ready to be pressed into extra duty as a prop in teaching. Suspenders held up his beltless pants. When he went out, a beret covered his sparse white hair.

At our first meeting, the slightly built five-foot-five-musician looked so fragile, yet moved so gracefully. Watching his intense eyes that shone with such depth, I said to myself, "Here is a precious man – a child of God!"

On the night of the first class, in early December, the weather could not have been more uncomfortable for him; it was a drizzly, icy bone-chiller.

As the appointed students took their turns to play, I sat spellbound as his wisdom, good humor, and spirit enveloped each one of them.

At the end of this exciting three-hour master class, I went backstage to meet Mr. Moyse. He was completely surrounded by inspired students. After they reluctantly parted, he was left alone—with no other faculty members in sight.

After introducing myself, I inquired, "Is someone coming to drive you to your hotel?"

His reply was, "I don't know – I don't see anyone."

"Please come with me, I would be honored", I said.

Unfortunately, my vehicle was a Volkswagen van, with a very high step up to the front seat. Here was a man, nearly 80 years old, weighing 110 lbs. recovering from major surgery – the removal of his stomach.

Conditions were icy and wet and I knew that I had to help as I saw him struggling to lift his foot high enough to reach the step.

I said to him, "We'll have to work together, OK?"

He put his arms around me, and I surprisingly lifted him onto the front seat.

That was a humbling experience for both of us.

When we got to the hotel and went to his room, I received the wonderful gift of meeting "Mimi," his dear, charming wife of 50 years. She was matronly looking but graceful in movements. She possessed the sparkle of a person who was totally engaged in life.

"Whoever travels without a guide needs two hundred years for a two-day journey."

Rumi

HOW HE WORKED

Oberlin Conservatory faculty had no understanding of how Mr. Moyse worked. They wanted to confine him to a narrow schedule, one hour here, one hour there. However, he came from the Paris Conservatory tradition, and it was his style to conduct a class or a lesson until he was exhausted—classes often ended several hours after they began. He vociferously expressed his frustration to the faculty. On his second day of seminars, he was moved to the large choral room, teaching Paris Conservatory style nightly from 7pm until <u>everyone</u> was exhausted.

Moyse taught by analogy, by musical example, by his personality, often using his own books of exercises. He called his unique method of teaching "The naturelle way." Whatever the students' level of expertise and spirit in seeking his wisdom, he loved working with them all; he absorbed their exuberance and healing energy.

"The Master Finds the Pupil."

Musc Najib

HE INVITED HIMSELF FOR LUNCH

By the second day of Moyse's visit, the faculty at Oberlin showered him with many invitations for lunches, dinners and receptions. He refused them all. It was not his style to be "the famous guest." (Besides, after his experience that first night, he keenly felt the faculty's lack of interest in his teaching and the lack of preparation for his classes, i.e., <u>not</u> making available his principal teaching books at the music store. He was furious.)

However, **in** the middle of a Woodwind class, Mr. Moyse suddenly stopped mid-sentence, looked in my direction and motioned with his finger that I should come to him.

He whispered in my ear, "I worked with the faculty woodwind quintet today."

"Your husband plays <u>beeuuteefullly</u> (beautifully)!"

"I and my wife are coming to your house for lunch on Friday at 1:30."

"I can eat potatoes, soup, bread, and bananas, and I drink tea with sugar."

On the appointed day and time, I served potato soup with bread, a fruit bowl and of course the tea with sugar. After lunch, Marcel and Mimi settled back on the sofa, and he lit his pipe. Soon, his head was totally hidden in the smoke.

After a while, he asked me to play for them. I was prepared for this eventuality. I was a talented flutist, I had been taught well by University of Michigan Professor, Nelson Hauenstein, a very dear and generous teacher who inspired in me a natural warm tone and the ability to produce a wide repertoire.

I played two unaccompanied flute pieces, one by Debussy, the other by J.S. Bach for Mr. Moyse. My performance would have pleased Professor Hauenstein.

Marcel turned to Mimi and said, "You see, I told you she is the best!"

"Fine," I said.

But the truth became clear in my future lessons with him that I had actually only accomplished the first step toward bringing the composers' music to life with my flute.

MY FOUR HOUR LESSON

I went to West Brattleboro, Vermont, as often as finances and motherhood allowed for private lessons with Mr. Moyse.

One particular visit occurred during a wonderful "January Thaw." The sky was a beautiful clear blue and the melting snow sparkled in the sunshine. People stopped work, threw off their overcoats (but not their boots) and all the outdoor lunch spots were filled with people enjoying the winter break!

I trudged up the long steep hill to Mr. Moyse's Vermont chalet (passing a farm horse with long thick fur hanging down about four inches from his body).

The lesson started at 2 pm. I had prepared the Allemande from J.S. Bach's *Unaccompanied Flute Sonata in A Minor*. I also brought Mr. Moyse's published *50 Variations on the Allemande*, which he had composed to facilitate understanding of the Bach work, and to help the player discover natural phrasing and breathing points, in a piece of unrelenting sixteenth notes. Four hours later, I finished playing all 50 variations, including #50, the "jazz" variation.

At the end of the lesson, Le Maitre stood up. His arms shot straight up as he stamped his foot joyfully, with "HAA! You improve leet by leet (little by little). Silver flute, golden tone."

Twenty minutes later, I arrived at my hotel—as if in a dream—to rest on my bed for a few moments before dinner. I woke up at 10 AM the next day!!

PART TWO –
STORIES MOYSE TOLD
ABOUT HIS LIFE

WHERE'S THE BEAT?

THE AUDITION

"I DIDN'T KNOW MY ETUDE
COULD BE SO BEAUTIFUL!"

DEDICATION AND REVELATION

CRESCENDO!

SHIPS PASSING IN THE NIGHT

PROBLEM SOLVED

THE FOUNDING OF MARLBORO
MUSIC FESTIVAL

A MUSICAL JOKE

"AS THE WORLD TURNS"

F SHARP

"For me, the rhythm is the <u>most</u> important in music."

Marcel Moyse

WHERE'S THE BEAT?

Moyse was trying to get a student to show the rhythm clearly (in that case, upbeats to downbeats). He stopped to recall that as a young orphan, living at his uncle's house near Besancon Conservatory (where his uncle taught cello), he would often be practicing downstairs. At times, he would be interrupted by the sound of a cane banging on the floor above his head.

" Marcel, where's the beat?" his uncle shouted through the floor. "The highest note is not on the strong beat."

Years later, Marcel got his "revenge." When he heard his uncle's cello student upstairs playing a triplet passage with an ambiguous beat, he pounded on the ceiling and called, " Uncle, where's the beat?"

"It don't mean a thing if it ain't got that swing."
Duke Ellington

"Never trouble trouble till trouble troubles you!"

Anonymous

THE AUDITION

Marcel Moyse was 16-years-old when he auditioned for Paris Conservatory in 1905. The faculty jury included awe-inspiring composers and performers, such as Taffanel, Franck, Saint-Saens, Thomas and Massanet.

He often described his many weeks of intense preparation for this terrifying event. Every day while he practiced, he imagined walking into the audition room and performing for this illustrious Board, all seated at a long table, wearing frowning faces.

"When the audition day came," he said, " I decided not to warm up in the flute room where I knew that all of the flute players in the room would intimidate me with their incredible warm-up routines."

"Instead, I decided that my first note that day would be for the Board. I went directly to the doorman and told him to call me when it was my time to play. Later, when I entered the audition room, a very unexpected thing happened to me – suddenly, I was no longer nervous!" His powerful imagination conjured up an experience that proved to be far worse than the actual one!

He often admonished his students, "Don't associate with other flutists!"

"Every composer deserves the same effort, the same respect to every detail."

Marcel Moyse

"Practice being nervous!"

Marcel Moyse

"I DIDN'T KNOW MY ETUDE COULD BE SO BEAUTIFUL!"

- Joachim Andersen

"The music has a life of its own. I try to let it come through,"

Marcel Moyse

Mr. Moyse regarded Andersen's music as "our Chopin for the flute." He related his teacher, Taffanel's experience of performing Andersen's *Etude* Opus. 15, No. 3. (1905)

"Joachim Andersen was sitting at a table in front of Taffanel," Moyse told me, "with his face down on his folded arms, listening motionlessly. After a little silence, Andersen slowly raised his head. Tears were streaming down his face and he said, 'I never knew my music could be so beautiful.'"

(When I was studying Andersen's *Etude* with Moyse, practicing first the underlying melody, the tonal quality mysteriously attracted my Collie, Taffy. Whenever I played that melody at home, she always jumped up and put her paws lovingly on my shoulders.)

FROM DEDICATION TO REVELATION

"For many years, I dedicated my life as a flutist to playing and sounding exactly like Taffanel—my teacher at Paris Conservatory.

"I put myself totally into my teacher's hands, but I learned too well and too fast. In fact, I was disappointed to graduate, receiving my First Prize after only one short school year. I was not ready to leave Taffanel because I wanted to learn MORE."

Although Moyse was completely immersed in his journey to become like Taffanel, one day, years later, he suddenly realized that he was <u>not</u> another Taffanel, but that he was Moyse, and, "it wasn't bad!"

"If Taffanel were alive today," he once declared to a flute class assembled in his Vermont home, "I would go on my knees all the way to Philadelphia to take lessons from him again." (June 1975)

CRESCENDO!

Mr. Moyse told our flute class at his chalet in Brattleboro the following story.

"I had an Italian houseguest who spoke no French. I spoke no Italian.

'Early one morning, we took a car to a scenic spot in the Jura Mountains to watch the sunrise.

'We were overcome by the beauty of the moment. Spontaneously, the Italian shouted, "CRESCENDO!"

SHIPS PASSING IN THE NIGHT

Mr. Moyse often reminisced about his wonderful eight-month concert tour in 1913 with the famous Australian coloratura soprano, Nellie Melba. They toured Canada and the United States, starting in Montreal and ending in San Diego. He was in his glory, playing flute solos and duets with the soprano, developing richly as a solo performer (a rare opportunity for flutists those days), while enjoying a real high point in his career. (This tour became the beginning of a new era—the first time in history that a concert flutist became a soloist. As the decades passed, Rampal, Galway and many others followed Moyse's lead.)

When the tour ended, he was out of work and sorely disappointed that a new orchestra position in Minnesota that had been promised him did not materialize. Meanwhile, his beloved wife, Mimi, was obliged to wait in France for his employment to improve.

Moyse told me that he and Mimi desperately missed each other. In frustration, he went to a pawnshop with his only flute (a cheap, unattractive instrument) to see if he could sell it to buy passage to Le Havre. Attempting to sell the flute, he performed a magnificent little concert for the highly skeptical pawnbroker. He said to me, "I never played so well in my life!" The pawnbroker was so impressed that he paid Marcel several times more than the basic value of the instrument. Alas, this incredible concert gained him only partial passage to France, and he had to clean horse stables most of the way to make up the full fare.

In the meantime, Mimi, who was also lonely for him, somehow found the money to book passage on a ship to New York with their small son, Louis. And yes, Mimi and Marcel crossed in the middle of the ocean!

Moyse's flute showed up again sometime later, owned by a new student. To buy it back, he paid the student a great deal more than he had sold it for to the pawnbroker.

One might wonder why a musician would get so attached to one particular instrument. Scientific experiments (by mid-20th century clarinetist Daniel Bonade) have concluded that sound-wave patterns are formed inside the metal or wood tube or barrel that are unique to the owner. In effect, the musician "trains" the instrument to produce his/her unique qualities of sound; and the instrument becomes more and more precious to him/her. When hearing a real artist, one feels like the player and the instrument are one.

"Everything is simpler than you think,
and more complex than you imagine."

Goethe

PROBLEM SOLVED

Moyse often told the following story to his classes.

A colleague of his, named Georges Laurant, played first flute in Boston Symphony under Koussevitzky, starting in the mid 1920's. The orchestra was rehearsing a Mahler symphony which required a low B in the flute part. Unfortunately, Laurant did not have the B extension on his instrument; C was his lowest note. (Few flutes at that time were made with a B foot.) Koussevitzky stopped the orchestra. "Where's the B? I need that B," he said. Laurant valiantly tried to explain the situation but he had no success at all.

That night he borrowed a B foot from another flutist. The next day at rehearsal he was able to produce the B. Koussevitzky abruptly stopped the orchestra and said, "There, you see what a little practice can do!"

THE FOUNDING OF MARLBORO MUSIC FESTIVAL

In 1949, concert pianist Rudolph Serkin wrote to Moyse, saying that there was a small college town in Vermont, near Serkin's country farm home, needing a music faculty. He suggested that the Moyse Trio could become the entire faculty. This trio was well-known as an illustrious European performing group: Moyse could teach flute and chamber music; Louis, his son, could teach composition and piano; and Blanche Honneger Moyse, his daughter-in-law, could teach violin, music courses and conduct choirs.

The Moyse family graciously took his suggestion and once again packed all of their belongings. From Argentina, they sailed to New York where they were met and taken to Marlboro, Vermont. A house had been rented for them. The setting pleased the Moyse family enormously, and they were inspired by the similarity of the Green Mountains in Vermont to the Jura Mountains in France. They also found the climate to be refreshingly similar.

By the summer of 1950, Rudolph Serkin, pianist, Adolph Busch, cellist, and Marcel Moyse were joyfully playing chamber music together. News of their informal playing spread and musicians began to gather. Their numbers grew from a few selected students and musicians to crowds who found housing accommodations in succeeding summers on the Marlboro College campus.

As more prominent musicians joined the original three, the philosophy they held was one of mix and match. For example, mature seasoned professionals (often famous), joined those in mid career, along with musicians entering the profession. They loved the democratic atmosphere they had created, as they freely played together and learned from each other. The atmosphere there became a kind of utopia. Students came in droves to hear their teachers perform informal summer concerts, which officially started in 1951.

Concerts were originally held in the college dining hall and later in a converted barn.

During mealtimes, the dining hall, filled with musicians and their families, often became a melee of napkin ball fights, usually started by Rudolph Serkin.

Over the years, the festival attracted bigger and bigger crowds; performances/recordings changed the focus to big business. Marvelous music continued to be produced. The arrival of cellist Pablo Casals added more fame to the festival. At the same time, Moyse drew too many flutists and woodwind players for Marlboro to accommodate; so he held seminars for winds, pre-season, beginning in 1961. He was also loved as a fantastic conductor of large woodwind works that were performed at festival concerts. Historical recordings are available.

A MUSICAL JOKE - 1968

A package tour of concert fans arrived on a bus in Marlboro, VT, and wandered into the famous "Barn." (They were looking forward to hearing a concert there that evening.) Mr. Moyse was conducting and coaching a flute quartet. The flutist, violinist, violist and cellist were working on the Mozart *Flute Quartet in D*. K V 285, second movement.

Glancing sideways, Moyse whispered to the 6'7" flutist named Ornolf Gulbransen (from Oslo, Norway) that they could have some fun and that he should follow Moyse's "suggestions."

The quartet began the second movement. After the first phrase, Moyse stopped them and pointed to Gulbranson shaking his finger, "No, No, Gulbransen, <u>show</u> the quick notes. Start again." The flutist at that point lifted slightly off his chair, wiggled his butt and sat down again with no interruption to the music.

The musicians started again. "No, No, show that you went <u>up</u>!" So, Gulbransen wiggled, stood up and sat down.

They played again. "You have to lean on the dissonance." With that, Gulbransen nearly fell out of his chair on the dissonant notes. For trills, he quivered as much as he could without disrupting the music. On the syncopated leap, he jumped three feet off the floor, along with Moyse!

After various maneuvers throughout the movement, Gulbransen ended up sitting on top of the piano!

"That man is richest whose pleasures are the cheapest."

Thoreau

"AS THE WORLD TURNS" (1971)

I experienced Moyse's wild spirit as a passenger in his car. He started out like a jackrabbit leaping out of a hole, then remembered that I was there and attempted to control his driving. As we sped along, talking amiably, he threw caution to the wind and resumed driving like a maniac. I enjoyed the adventure of driving with Le Maitre.

Over the years, Moyse drove huge distances, often at breakneck speed, and often overnight, to get to his studios in Montreal, Boston and New York. After driving all night, he would teach during the day, then get back into his car and drive again to his home in Vermont, or to his next destination in the triangle.

Postcard to me with a personal
letter on the reverse side, 1969.

Loving speed as he did, his "expressive driving" earned him many citations and several suspensions. His driver's license was always returned to him, until he had a dreaded moment when he backed into a student's car and was forced to surrender his license—for good.

Moyse felt deeply the enormous loss of freedom to come and go as he pleased. However, watching a TV soap, hand in hand with his wife after lunch, became a consolation as he became more and more emotionally involved with the characters and plot. "As the World Turns" became his window on the world, and he often regarded the actors as though they were part of his family.

As Mr. Moyse's designated driver, I waited respectfully by his door every day until the TV episode was finished to drive him to his class at St. Michael's Church in Brattleboro. As we drove, we were always immersed in a lively debate about a particular character's fate and moral consequences, and were frequently surprised that we arrived at our destination so soon!

F SHARP (1972))

Moyse had just finished telling a very silly joke when Mimi walked by the class with an amused smile. He rolled his heavy office chair, with its familiar rumble, over to her and slapped her on the tusch. Hearing that resonating tone, he turned to the class and said, "F Sharp!"

Mimi turned back with a toss of her head and a tolerant twinkle.

PART THREE –
JANUARY 1981, NEWPORT
BEACH, CA

PIED PIPER

"I JUST DISCOVERED SOMETHING"

GRUELING SCHEDULE

LOST MOYSE MANUSCRIPT
(PUBLISHER'S ALERT)

DAY OFF AT DANA POINT

DER FREICHUTZ

THE REAL PRIORITY

PILGRIMAGE TO THE CORONADO

PIED PIPER

The following photograph and article appeared in the Newport Beach *Daily Pilot* newspaper in January 1981.

Pied Piper

Playing the flute is like singing into a silver tube,
says 92-year-old master flutist Marcel Moyse

By JUDITH OLSON

Marcel Moyse, reputedly one of the greatest flute players in the world, is 92 now and there's a sense of urgency about talking with him. There are all sorts of questions to be asked, a lifetime of experience to be culled for tidbits for tomorrow. What makes a good flute player? How does Moyse produce special sounds on his flute that have been called "warm?" And what is this business of playing the flute all about, anyway?

Moyse, a Frenchman who has spent much of his life in Vermont, speaks English but tosses in a few French words from time to time. Coupled with his slowed speech, his French/English is sometimes difficult to understand. But with gestures and taps with his ever-present pipe, Moyse makes his point.

He's a man of great humor. He laughs at the world and at himself with equal fervor, delighting his friends who then admire him the more.

MOYSE SAYS the flute is an extension of the human body and that the instrument by itself is nothing. "I sing through the instrument," he said. Vibration is one of the keys to good music, he added, illustrating his point by tapping his coffee cup with his pipe and then hitting the same cup with his hand, absorbing the sound.

Moyse teased that his own body is like a flute since he has had nine operations recently. "Here's a hole and here's a hole and here's another," he pointed with a grin, letting his whimsical wit show through.

The master flutist, in Southern California to teach at the University of Southern California, California Institute of the Arts and Mount Saint Mary's College, was visiting one of his students, Susan Fries, for a month. He supposedly had come for a vacation, but had written music every day during his stay in Newport Beach, Ms. Fries said.

HE SEEMS TO have a difficult time understanding a question about his philosophy of music. What makes a good flutist as opposed to simply a musician? "It's a gift that has to be developed," he said. "But it also takes intelligence."

Moyse is exact about his art, however. "Each note has a different coloring," he writes in one of his numerous books about the technical aspects of playing the flute. He believes making the flute work is simply extending the movement of the human body. It's singing into a silver tube, putting all the human emotions into the tones of the instrument.

The master, who has been close friends with many great names in music, including composers Stravinsky and Ravel and conductors Walter and Stokowski, said music is a good way to link the world. "There is no nationality to music," he said.

"I JUST DISCOVERED SOMETHING!!"

Every morning, while visiting me in Newport Beach, Mr. Moyse was totally immersed in practicing. Early one morning, he suddenly opened the door, rushed out with a youthful eagerness in his wide eyes and exclaimed, "I JUST DISCOVERED SOMETHING!"

I was astonished to think that at 92 years old, having played the flute from age nine, he was still discovering new aspects of his art!

I am grateful to him every day of my life that he awakened in me the love for the flute and opened the gate to the continual discoveries that keep my playing and teaching exciting.

"The one thing genuine artists put aside for their old age is the thought of retirement."

Anonymous

GRUELING SCHEDULE

Throughout the month of January, 1981, while Moyse stayed with me in Newport Beach, California, he asked for a small bedroom in my home. He wanted the room to be heated to at least 80 degrees, and contain only a bed, a desk with chair, and good lighting. (During his stay with me, he took only one day off, while working at a pace that I, at a much younger age found difficult to match.)

His daily schedule was:

5 AM-10AM: Writing, breakfast, shower, etc.
10:45-12:45: Practice flute
12:45: Drive to Los Angeles
2 PM: Flute Master Class
5:30: Dinner
7:30-10 PM: Woodwind Master Class
11 PM: Home, visit with my sons.
12 AM: Bed.

At this time, Moyse was writing a book, devoted to solving specific technical and musical problems for flutists in orchestral and solo repertoire. He had been working on this project for several hours a day for almost three years.

When I traveled to his Flute and Woodwind Classes later that spring, he was still very involved in writing this manuscript; he was at that point trying out ideas and examples on his students.

1984: Tragically, during the last year of his life, this last manuscript was stolen. This loss of six years labor was a crushing blow to Moyse. He died three months later. Because of the great concern of his family, friends, colleagues and students, the following notice appeared in *The Flutist Quarterly*, Summer, 1985:

LOST MOYSE MANUSCRIPT
Publisher's Alert

After Marcel Moyse's last seminars in June 1984 in Brattleboro, Vermont, the manuscript for a new book he was writing was discovered to be missing. The new book had no title, was on loose sheets of large size music paper, and had been in preparation for the past six years. It is written in his own precise and unmistakable handwriting, and represents countless hours of detailed and careful work, in addition to being his final contribution in a long line of invaluable books for the flutist. To show the importance of certain notes, some were notated in red ink, while the rest were in black. Needless to say, Mr. Moyse was most upset to have found it missing, and Blanche Moyse [his daughter-in-law] is making every effort to recover it.

If you have the manuscript, perhaps enclosed unwittingly in your own music, please mail it to:

Mrs. Blanche Moyse
South Street
West Brattleboro, VT
05301

No questions asked.

If you have any information leading to its recovery, please notify Blanche Moyse. If you are a publisher presented with this material for publication, take note of its history: it may be stolen property.

Post Script: To my knowledge, the manuscript has never been found. Nonetheless, some people in the music world believe that it exists in various forms today; pieces of Moyse's cherished work have been published as parts of other people's works.

DAY OFF AT DANA POINT

On Moyse's one day off, during the entire month he stayed with me, I suggested that we drive south along the coast from Corona del Mar, through Laguna Beach to Dana Point. Le Maitre sat comfortably on a pillow in the front seat, drinking in the scenic beauty and the delicious ocean air. His daughter-in-law companion, Blanche Moyse, was relieved to have a free day to explore and enjoy Southern California sunshine and the Pacific Ocean. (Without Blanche, Moyse could not have made the trip to California.)

We drove around the arms of Dana Point Harbor, stopping to watch the boats and enjoy the weather. The 3 o'clock hour was approaching and that meant whiskey time for Moyse. So I drove us up to a wonderful restaurant perched on the top of the cliff above the harbor. The seating was low and the view was spectacular through the floor to ceiling windows. We even caught sight of several migrating whales.

The young waitress came to take our orders. Moyse's fascinated eyes slowly scanned her up and down, and up and down again. Her skirt stopped just at the edge of her panties!

As she walked away, he said with delight and a mischievous little twinkle, " I hope she doesn't trip on her skirt! "

DER FRIESCHUTZ!

My daughter, Laura (now a singer with the Metropolitan Opera), was a freshman at the University of Southern California, Los Angeles, the year Moyse stayed with me.

One day, she was practicing "Und ob die Wolke" from Der Freischutz while accompanying herself on the piano. Moyse said, "Repetez, s`il vous plait." He then asked her to repeat the aria five times.

He loved the many qualities of her voice and musicianship and just couldn't get enough of the beauty of this aria.

Marcel asked Blanche sometime later, "Do I have this melody in *Tone Development through Interpretation?*" (This book is his superb collection of 90 favorite melodies—gathered over 43 years—from opera, ballet, symphony, and chamber music scores. He used it to teach expression, tonal colors and characters in flute playing. Players also used these melodies to develop expression and tonal colors with Moyse in woodwind seminars,)

He told me many times to be open—to learn not only from other flutists—but to learn also from singers, cellists, violinists, pianists, pantomime artists, nature, and from human drama.

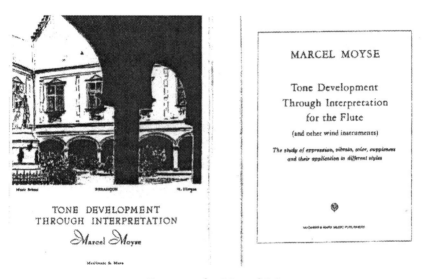

Cover art by Marcel Moyse

" I don't care where you bought your flute – Where can I buy your lips?"

Marcel Moyse

THE REAL PRIORITY (1981)

During January 1981, Mr. Moyse was approached many times by several flute companies that were trying to have his endorsement of their flutes. Their representatives proposed to make magnificent top of the line flutes, built completely to Moyse's specifications. Alternatively, they suggested creating an exact reproduction of his flute (to which several appendages had been added to make it what he laughingly called his "orthopedic" flute).

Moyse did not believe that flutists should depend on a particular brand of flute to create beautiful music. He preferred not to "endorse" any flute. He remarked one day, "I do not ask you <u>where</u> you bought your instrument, I ask you, <u>where</u> can I buy your leeps (lips)?"

During the 15 years that I knew and worked with Le Maitre, he talked to me about companies that were developing flutes with "designer" tones. This trend worried him; he believed that while the new hi-tech flutes greatly improved intonation, they also made it possible for "seven out of 10 flutists" to easily produce good tones. He was concerned that the development of these flutes helped to create lazy flutists who didn't bother to produce distinctive tone qualities. He wondered if flute companies would take all of the credit for their beautiful tones. (Mr. Moyse often commented that during the early 1900's, only three out of 10 players produced good tones.) He preferred his old Cousenon, because he could create more nuances in color and character.

While listening to the re-mastered recordings of Marcel Moyse, I realize that many times he became so passionate and excited that his flute could not contain his energy; his intonation sounded very sharp at times. (In the early 20th century, before modern developments in flutes, poor intonation in concerts and recordings was commonly excused.)

PILGRIMAGE TO THE CORONADO

Marcel, Blanche and I enjoyed a few delicious meals at a seafood restaurant overlooking the beautiful Newport Bay. At one meal, he drifted into a reverie about being a very happy young man on tour, performing "at the sea" in San Diego. He had stayed at the Coronado Hotel (built in 1888), renowned for its historic splendor and location on vast white sand beaches.

Moyse had toured through the United States and Canada for eight months in 1913, with Nellie Melba, the great coloratura soprano. He recalled playing flute parts in Donizetti's *Mad Scene* from *Lucia di Lammermoor*, *Sweet Bird* from Handel's *IL Pensieroso* and others, and completing concerts with various solo pieces for the flute. His approach to playing was to always produce tone that had qualities approaching the singing voice. I can only imagine the spectacular blend of these two performers.

After he completed teaching the Los Angeles master classes, he made a special pilgrimage from my home in Newport Beach to The Coronado Hotel, 90 miles away. He wanted to relive the precious memories of that joyous time in his musical life.

PART FOUR – THE FLUTE CLASS: 1967 – 1981

AN INSPIRATIONAL FLUTE CLASS
WHAT CAN I DO (I AM SO NERVOUS)
THE PRONOUNCEMENT
OBJECTIVITY
WHO IS THE COMPOSER, ANYWAY?
PIECE POUR FLUTE SEULE
FOUR KINDS OF STUDENTS
"HE DOESN'T CARE!"
HUNGARIAN FANTASY
SCALES
"THE SECRET IS UP THERE ON THE LEFT!"
PURGATORY
EMPHASIS
"HAVE YOU EVER BEEN IN LOVE?"
SIMPLICITY
ATMOSPHERE
THE POWER OF SILENCE
THE BEE
ELEPHANT OR THE FLEA?
TEACHER'S EMBARASSING MOMENT
TWO MEN ON A TRAIN
AMAZING GRACE
"…BUT, MR. MOYSE, ARE YOU EVER SERIOUS?"
PROPORTION

"The job of the artist is always
to deepen the mystery."

Francis Bacon

AN INSPIRATIONAL FLUTE CLASS

The first professional flutist had finished playing the allegro scherzando, third movement of the Jacques Ibert *Concerto for Flute and Orchestra*. This movement is an incredible technical challenge with its triplets at mm ♩=176! (I once heard Jean-Pierre Rampal perform this movement. He began at tempo, but quickly overtaken by his ego, he gleefully accelerated to the point of leaving the poor orchestra far behind.) Coming out of his usual reverie, Moyse suddenly exploded into solfege, singing the part in tempo—as he demonstrated all of the motivic twists. Again, as the flutist continued, Le Maitre broke into song, this time adding important orchestral parts. Solfege, perfectly executed at that speed, is rare for any musician. I have never heard a performance anything like that.

Noticing the wonder in people's eyes, Moyse said that solfege was his way of life as a boy; he sang little songs, skipping in rhythm on his way home after school.

The second flutist to play was having difficulty with the Hüe *Fantasy*. After hearing the entire piece, Moyse asked to hear a melody with its variation from his *24 Petite Melodic Etudes*. He always welcomed and preferred these little compositions, rather than endure a participant's attempt to perform a work far beyond his/her ability—prepared to impress the teacher and colleagues. (These simple, elegant melodies are marvelous learning tools, written to bring out elements students had not thought of before, connecting them to the delicate subtleties of the musical language that even professional performers might not notice.) The aforementioned participant became so rich in sound and expression, one might think a different player had just arrived.

Flutist number three played the first movement of J.S. Bach's *Sonata No 1 in B Minor*. Moyse called the sub theme of the piece, illustrated below, the hurdy gurdy tune; he often heard organ grinders with dancing monkeys play this rhythmic little tune on the streets of Paris.

He worked with flutist number four on *De La Sonorite,* a deceptively simple method written by Moyse to help the flutist create a pure, beautiful, homogeneous tone (with exact intonation) throughout all registers. (The first tonal development exercise should culminate in a long silk thread of beautiful color – a smooth chromatic scale.) Moyse said he preferred to think of the ascending scale of the flute, from the lowest C to the highest C, as pink gradually turning to red; the transition should occur so gradually the listener could not tell when one color changed to the other.

When the day ended, the flutists and auditors slumped in their chairs, exhausted from striving to play their best. Some heads were hurting from learning new concepts, ways of articulating phrases clearly, creating vibrant tones, solving technical problems (by creating little exercises around them) and from increased understanding of musical structure.

At that point, La Maitre thrusted his arms into the air with a smile and symbolically congratulated all of the students. Then he relaxed, filled his pipe and offered them an anecdote from his life—a life that was filled with beautiful melodies.

The true teacher knocks down the idol that the student makes of him."

Rumi

WHAT CAN I DO?
(I AM SO NERVOUS)

A very popular flutist, known for his beautiful tone, had come to Vermont to work with The Master. He was a wonderful principal flutist, having performed for many years in a major U.S. orchestra. He also had a fine reputation as a teacher and had brought some of his best students to participate in Moyse's flute class.

When this flutist's turn came, he got short of breath, faltered and broke down in the middle of the short melody with variation that he had selected from Moyse's book, *24 Short Melodies with Variations.*

The poor man was in tears. Many of us shared his tears with quiet empathy.

"Le Maitre, I am so nervous I cannot play the way I want to," he said.

Moyse paused quietly. "Do you think I am *not* nervous? I am so scared that I will tell you wrong things!"

The two men's eyes met, they hugged for a few moments, and then the student relaxed. They had an inspiring workout together! The teacher and the player produced the teaching.

"What is a beautiful tone? Nobody knows—that is what you decide."

Marcel Moyse

THE PRONOUNCEMENT (1968)

I was attending a flute class during the late sixties—a time when hippies were proliferating in Vermont. At the beginning of the class, Moyse abruptly stood up to give an important announcement.

"I am a member of a <u>cult</u>!" he said with great emphasis.

The room was immediately hushed, followed by whispered confusion.

After a very theatrically long pause, he said,….. "The Cult of the Beautiful Tone!"

"'Mr. Moyse, I love your tone!' 'Which one?'"

"The greatest vanity is to believe that one is sincere in seeking knowledge when in reality one is seeking only personal pleasure."

Abu Halim Farfar

OBJECTIVITY (1973)

In Vermont, in the early 70's, an arrogant student strode up to Mr. Moyse at the class break.

"How would you like to have me as a student,?" he inquired jauntily, assuming that the teacher would be thrilled at the prospect.

Moyse gazed at him through the cloud of pipe smoke surrounding his head, and retorted, "...No."

SHOCK..SILENCE.

Moyse could be endlessly patient with a sincere, intelligent student who played a simple melody or etude (he especially liked Andersen or Soussman) or a piece well within the flutist's ability. He believed that all flutists should be able to play Tulou, the composer who lit our way to the real interpretation of Mozart! He became furious with a student who played to impress—to "show off"—with no intention to listen or to learn. The composer's music and the teacher's wisdom and guidance had been disrespected.

However, when Le Maitre began to work with a sincere student, the world dropped away, and he became totally engaged in the process of teaching until he was exhausted. (A lesson could be one hour or several.)

"The position of the artist is humble.
He is essentially a channel."

Piet Mondrian

WHO IS THE COMPOSER ANYWAY? (1972)

A student named Williams was performing the beautiful solo piece, *Syrinx,* by Claude Debussy.

Mr. Moyse was sitting quietly with his eyes closed, facing the window throughout the entire performance. His face was so expressionless that some people wondered if he was sleeping. I had already learned through experience that he heard everything, although he didn't appear to be listening.

When she finished playing the piece, Moyse sat and meditated for a while. Then he asked her, "Who is the composaire?"

She said, of course, "Debussy."

Moyse said, "Then, this is not the Williams' Fantasy?"

She responded, "No!"

"Respect the compasaire! Begin again."

This time, he insisted that every rhythm, as well as every dynamic and detail of every nuance that the composer had written, must be accurately executed. It had to be performed perfectly, he said. When Ms. Williams finally performed it correctly, she was at the beginning of an incredible transformation. The real Debussy was coming to life.

The accurate interpretation of a composition is an extremely difficult undertaking—much more difficult than most musicians realize. To understand the markings and give them life requires a great deal of imagination—not to be a slave to the composer, but to be the voice of the composer.

I also heard him say that he knew and worked with Debussy for 20 years, and that Debussy constantly told players to play what he wrote—exactly!

Always be true to the composer!

Marcel Moyse

"To make clear the form, the structure is built brick by brick, then the quality of feeling, the genuineness, yes the purity of feeling. Great composers are not stereotypes."

Marcel Moyse

PIECE POUR FLUTE SEULE (1972)

In the course of that "Syrinx" class, Le Maitre told the following story.

He was invited to the French Embassy reception in Prague after his premier performance of the Ibert *Concerto* in 1937. The hostess asked Moyse to bring his flute to entertain the guests.

The honored composer/conductor, Jacques Ibert, attended the reception. In tribute to Moyse, this brilliant musician composed a little solo piece for him (Ibert said he had composed the piece in less than an hour). Ibert gave the manuscript to Moyse and directed him to play all of the rhythms, dynamics, articulations and nuances, exactly as written!

The piece was gorgeously performed by a great flutist.

Can you imagine sight-reading this piece for an illustrious crowd?

91

"The trouble with most of us is that we would rather be ruined by praise than saved by criticism."

Norman Vincent Peale

"You practice four hours a day and then you think you are a great artist...It is easier to play fancy and difficult than it is to make the effort to be a great artist!"

Marcel Moyse

FOUR KINDS OF STUDENTS

As I studied with Moyse over the years, I discovered that he had four kinds of students:

1. People who worshiped Moyse as though he was a guru or god.

2. People who thought of themselves as perfect and great and wanted to add the name Moyse to their resumes.

3. People who came to class to socialize, discuss flute brands, mouthpieces and head joints. After staying up into the wee hours, they would arrive yawning the following day. It became clear that their degree of development allowed only the enjoyment of Moyse's jokes and entertainment, leaving the depth of his teaching above their heads.

4. People who recognized him as a real master of the flute and a gifted teacher who possessed the highest calling as a musician and person. Those students were ready and willing to put themselves totally in his hands.

Moyse, who would never dream of calling himself a master (although he knew his value), was well aware of the different types of students who came to his classes. He sometimes tested their sincerity with jokes, instructions or questions. He knew instantly if they were there for the entertainment or to obtain genuine understandings of the language of music.

In the case of an arrogant "show-off" student, Moyse became enraged and stormed out of the room, spewing strong expletives—returning 10 minutes later after he had cooled off.

"Real learning comes about when the competitive spirit has ceased."

J. Krishnamurti

"HE DOESN'T CARE!"

I was astounded to recognize that Moyse's stories, jokes and analogies always applied perfectly to specific musical problems.

A pleasant but untalented man, performing every note and rhythm correctly, had little expression or warmth in his playing. The result was boring! Moyse took a few moments to tell a few funny stories, hoping that they would help the student loosen up.

The student was asked to play his piece again.

No change.

Mr. Moyse told several additional stories and jokes, trying different approaches.

Finally he asked, "Are you married?"

The student replied, "Yes."

He played again with still no change.

"Do you love your wife?" asked Moyse.

"Yes, very much!"

Squeezing his arm, Mr. Moyse said, "If you do not make expression, I will KEEL (kill) your wife!"

He played again. No change.

"HE DOESN'T CARE!" Moyse retorted loudly. With that roguish statement, he could no longer contain himself and burst out laughing.

The class broke into such contagious roll-in-the-aisle laughter, that the poor student helplessly joined in, laughing the loudest of all.

"Good musicians execute their music but bad ones murder it."

Anonymous

'WAKE THE SLEEPING PEOPLE!"

Marcel Moyse

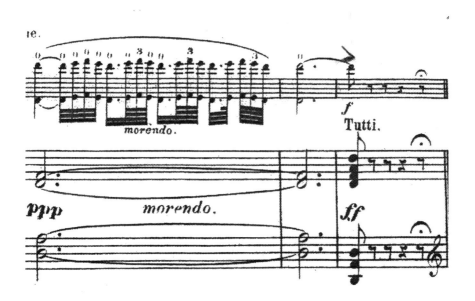

HUNGARIAN FANTASY

It was especially delightful to study the *Fantasie Pastorale Hongroise* Opus 26 by Albert Franz Doppler because Mr. Moyse performed so many "tricks" to get the composer's characters to come alive.

He would sometimes sing along with the player in a clear voice, adding a gravelly tone for drama in appropriate places.

His voice is memorable to me; it had a clear, sunny timbre.

I remember well how he would hide below the music stand and pop up at the appropriate moment for the sforzando (loud accent) necessary to "wake the sleeping people!"

In one part of the music, there is a peasant "dance." First, Moyse would do the man's dance with his hands behind his back, using great masculine footwork and turns. For the female version in the next section, with all of its turns and trills, he pulled out his handkerchief and fluttered it, adding delicate steps and turns on his toes. Then there was the big finish with the stamp of the foot, arms in the air, and the "HAAA!"

"*Success* comes before *work*—
only in the dictionary."

Anonymous

SCALES (1971)

Mr. Moyse arrived early. The Flute Master Class at St. Michael's Church in Brattleboro would start in a few minutes. After listening for several minutes to the sounds of people warming up, he pointed to a particular student who was practicing scales.

Mr. Moyse said, "Here is the student who is doing the most valuable practicing of all! Practice the G Major scale; <u>then</u> practice the Mozart *G Major Concerto*!" Most of the participating flutists incredulously thought that they were far beyond such mundane basics!

While on the subject of scales, in 1960, Pablo Casals, celebrating his 84th birthday, came to Marlboro to give a special master class. After tuning his cello, and reverently placing his bow on a string, he played a slow legato B minor scale. When he finished, he gently laid down his bow and said, "Wasn't that beautiful!"---and it <u>was</u>!

"The harder I work, the luckier I get."

Samuel Goldwyn

"THE SECRET IS UP THERE ON THE LEFT!"

A young woman was performing part of the Mozart *D Major Flute Concerto* for the class. Mr. Moyse was working with her assiduously, using many different methods to teach an important concept. He was getting more and more frustrated because she just didn't understand.

Finally, he picked up his flute and played the passage to illustrate what he meant. His tone and artistry were beautiful, colorful and full of life. He could have been the 22 year old.

After he finished playing, he leaned over and set down his old "clunker," (so named by an excellent Philadelphia woodwind repair man) which he had owned from age 14 or 15.

Casually laying the old flute on a side table next to his chair, Le Maitre turned back to the student. Instantly, there was an enormous rush as the whole class came up to the table to see his instrument.

Mr. Moyse was shocked…and amused. With a devilish look in his eyes, he held up his flute. Pointing, he said, " …..Oh, the secret is up there on the left!"

Jascha Heifitz also demonstrated this point, while visiting Oberlin Conservatory in 1968. Behind a screen, he played his famous Tononi violin, and then played a cheap " cigar box" violin. The audience could not tell which was which and even thought he had tricked them! He said, " The difference is that I have to work <u>extremely</u> hard to make the poor instrument sound good!"

"Simplicity is elegance."

Marcel Moyse

PURGATORY
(A well-known joke he often told)

Moyse told the class that he dreamed he had died.

"In this dream, I came to the big gates of heaven. Saint Peter asked who I was!

"'I am Marcel Moyse, a flutist. I believe God will remember that I played Mozart concertos quite well.'

"St. Peter said, 'Oh, Yes, Yes, come in......Mozart talked about you!'

"Then, I was led to a large lake full of shit. In the distance, I saw a man standing in it up to his chin. When I got closer, I realized that it was Schneider, the violinist who played Mozart with too many gypsy liberties.

"'Hello, Moyse,'

"'Hello, Schneider.'

"'Are you in purgatory too, Moyse?'

"'Yes, I think so. For how long will you be here?'

"'One hundred years!...and, you?'

"Six months. See, I told you to take care about Mozart. Ha. Ha. …….. And now, shall I dive or jump?

"Schneider cringed and yelled, 'PLEASE DON'T MAKE WAVES!'"

"When you play, you are an actor. You are creating the characters the composer called for."

Marcel Moyse

EMPHASIS

A student was struggling to make all the notes equally forceful. Of course her playing was not only heavy, it made no sense.

To illustrate the importance of phrasing with appropriate emphasis and punctuation, because music is a language, Moyse stopped her and related this humorous story:

"An 18 year old boy from a family of great actors was to audition for a touring repertory company. The line to prepare was, 'I come to the Cathedral of God.'

"This nervous young man went to his uncle for advice, and after delivering his line, was told, 'No, no! The important word is **I**, emphasize **I** come to the Cathedral of God.' "

"The Grandfather said it was **COME**. His father said it was **CATHEDRAL**. His mother said it was **GOD**."

"After consulting all of his mentors, the audition went like this: '**I - COME - TO - THE - CATHEDRAL - OF - GOD**!!!' Moyse gestured with a naughty laugh and said in a whisper, "….and he got the part!"

"Music is the language of love."

Marcel Moyse

"HAVE YOU EVER BEEN IN LOVE?" (1979)

A beautiful young woman was playing the exquisite *Andante in C*, by Mozart. Despite her physical beauty, her playing lacked expression and her tone was dull.

Moyse sat motionlessly in his chair by the window with his eyes closed as he usually did. After listening to the entire piece, he sat quietly looking out the window for a few moments.

"Have you ever been in love?" he asked.

She blushed and became speechless.

Then, with sudden pure delight and mischief in his 90-year-old eyes, he jumped up from his chair, threw his arms around her shoulders and squeezed, saying, "Well, if I were 50 years younger, I would SHOW you!"

Unfortunately, there was a young man in the group who took him literally. For the rest of our days in Vermont, he made a pest of himself as he tried to mimic Moyse's behavior with every girl in class. Sadly, he missed the real meaning of La Maitre's teaching.

"Simplicity is elegance—this is the best way to approach the performance of music— the simpler and purer it is, the better."

Marcel Moyse

"Everything should be made as simple as possible, but not simpler."

Albert Einstein

SIMPLICITY

Moyse occasionally received a postcard from his friend, Francis Poulenc. He remarked that those cards were composed of only one to four words. No more! But their meaning was perfect and told volumes, just as Poulenc's music does; every note is indispensable and nothing is superfluous.

"This is the best way to approach the performance of music—the simpler and purer it is, the better," Moyse always said. He was illustrating to the flute class that musical integrity means that as performers we simply must follow the composer's wishes, not our own flamboyance. The real beauty in playing comes from simple and pure intention.

"The music is sweet enough—Do not make it any sweeter!"

Marcel Tabuteau

"Think of how a flower or leaf vibrates with life—sometimes it has an almost imperceptible shimmer. Think of your tone that way."

Marcel Moyse

ATMOSPHERE (1972)

Moyse was gazing out of the big windows of his chalet in the Green Mountains near West Brattleboro, Vermont, where our flute class was assembled. We could see an early morning silvery blue mist hanging over the mountains. Some pine trees stood out in complete clarity and others receded in the mist.

"Create that blue atmosphere. Create the quality. Create the flavor. Create the serene mood in this beautiful melody," he said.

He raised his head and sniffed deeply, as if to smell the forest too. (Moyse was born without the ability to smell anything. "It could be *merde* or a rose," he would say, "I would not know the difference.")

One day, he excitedly told me that a student had just brought him a large bunch of violets and he thought he smelled them!

"Create atmosphere."

Marcel Moyse

A huge billiards table in the middle of Moyse's living/teaching room in his home was often stacked with piles of his many ongoing projects. A wooden bowl filled with a wonderful collection of pipes sat in the middle. Students familiar with his idiosyncrasies took this large obstacle in stride and arranged themselves around it.

In addition, a large grandfather clock chimed at inappropriate moments. We all tuned out the chiming and marveled at how we grew oblivious to it, in even the quietest moments.

Marcel Moyse

MARCEL MOYSE
MAY 17, 1889 - NOV 1ST 1984
ST. AMOUR FRANCE

THE POWER OF SILENCE

THE BEE

Mr. Moyse was energetically circling around a student, pointing his finger at her arm, buzzing like a bee. Circling closer and closer, he almost reached the student's arm and suddenly stopped dead. He made no sound or movement for two seconds. Then he touched the student's bristled arm.

"When you hear a bee buzzing, and getting closer to you, it is that silence before he stings that makes the sting so powerful; the same is true in music, the longer you wait, the stronger the impact (sfz) will be…HAA-unless you go too far!"

ELEPHANT OR THE FLEA?

"Which one has more energy, the elephant or the flea?" Moyse asked.

"The elephant!" was the hasty response of several people.

"Consider this: The flea can jump thousands of times his height, while the elephant cannot jump at all." He was saying that a staccato note must contain all the energy of a jumping flea!

TEACHER'S EMBARRASING MOMENT (1975)

Moyse told this story about one of his adventures in teaching.

"An older neighbor man wanted to learn to play the flute. Because Vermont winters are so long and isolating, he and I agreed to try.

"I struggled with him week after week to clear up an extremely rough tone. In fact, it sounded tee-reee-ble (terrible)! After several failures to make any progress, I thought the problem might be that the man was jamming the mouthpiece too hard on his lower lip."

"One day as the man was playing, I gently and slowly pulled the mouthpiece away from his mouth, intending to release pressure. To my astonishment and embarrassment, although his contact with the mouthpiece was completely gone, his ugly tone continued. The man had been buzzing and gargling into the flute the entire time!"

Mr. Moyse laughed heartily at his folly and was quickly joined by the class.

"The sound of laughter has always seemed to me the most civilized music in the universe."

Peter Ustinov

"In music one must think with the heart and feel with the brain."

George Szell

TWO MEN ON A TRAIN (1979)

A student was playing a beautiful melody, the <u>Arlesienne</u> by Bizet (#49 in *Tone Development through Interpretation).*

Moyse stopped him to illustrate the kind of emotional expression the composition called for by telling the student this story.

"Two soldiers were sitting side by side on a train. As the train left the station, the Italian, whose dog had run away, started to cry and moan profusely. Meanwhile, the Frenchman slowly took out his handkerchief and wiped away one tear. He was expressing a contained sensibility of grief over the death of his daughter.

"The Italian projects the emotion of the music outwardly with brilliant color and expansive drama. In contrast, the Frenchman creates a contained sensibility of color, nuance and atmosphere that radiates from his heart. Both expressions are powerful, but each is conveyed in a different way."

Mr. Moyse often told other stories of this type, using examples of contrasting emotions to fit a variety of musical dramas—for example, two lovers, a grandfather and granddaughter, etc.

"Without the heart, the brain cannot produce music."

Marcel Moyse

"The spirit and the will control the artist, not the obstacles."

Marcel Moyse

AMAZING GRACE (1979)

Moyse was slumped in his chair. (By the age of 90, he had endured nine major surgeries.) On that particular morning, he picked up his flute and started to gently improvise; this was always his way of warming up and of gradually working into the mood and character of the music he was preparing to play. Before our amazed eyes, he was becoming taller, straighter and younger looking.

His playing was exquisitely beautiful. He was living the music.

After a few minutes he put his flute on his lap and said, "When I play flute, I become a young boy… Now I am nine years old. I think I will be nine this year, nineteen next year, then 29, 39, 49 and so on." (He died at 59, according to his numbering system!)

About practicing, he said, "In a half hour, I change completely. I am a different man."

"What we play is the life!"
Marcel Moyse

"Great is the human who has not lost his childlike heart."
Mencius (Meng-Tse) (4th C. B.C.)

"…BUT, MR. MOYSE ARE YOU EVER SERIOUS?"

We were midway through an intensive ten-day Flute Seminar in Vermont in late June. On this particularly chilly morning, within the first few minutes of the class, we were already laughing heartily at Moyse's jokes, pantomimes and stories. As always, Le Maitre was intuitively using humor to create magnificent results in his students' playing.

At our 11:30 break, Mr. Moyse relaxed into his big comfortable leather chair and lit his pipe — one of his collection of more than 100 beautiful hand carved pipes that came from an artistic pipe maker who lived in the Jura Mountains of France.

A very serious English gentleman had become increasingly uncomfortable day after day with all of the lightness and humor in the class, not to mention the incredible transformation in the participants' performances.

On this morning, he could stand it no longer. He approached our beloved teacher with this question. "Mr. Moyse, are you <u>ever</u> serious?"

Moyse leaned back in his chair, his head encircled by a heavenly cloud of smoke, and became thoughtful. Suddenly, he came out of his reverie, leaned forward and replied definitively, "Yes, I am see-ree-oose (serious) about <u>one thing</u>!" as he shook his finger at the gentleman in time with his words, "Having <u>FUN</u> with mu-ZEEK (MUSIQUE).

PROPORTION (1968)

I was playing the J. S. Bach *Sonata No. I in B Minor* for Mr. Moyse at his home in West Brattleboro, Vermont. To illustrate a point about proportion, Mr. Moyse drew two profiles of Bach's head on the inside cover of my music score, one that looked like Bach and one that was out of proportion. He was illustrating that every note, ornament and expression must be true to the language of the composer and of the Baroque period. "Your playing should never be a caricature or distortion of the composer's intention. The melody should shine through."

Similarly, in flute classes, students sometimes performed baroque sonatas with overstated ornamentation. The ornaments were either played too loudly for the underlying phrases, or inappropriately for the Baroque period, or rhythmically disruptive to the phrase.

In one class, as a particular student finished playing a Bach sonata, Moyse sketched a beautifully proportioned racehorse; then he erased one knee and substituted a very large one with bulges all over it for one of the front legs to illustrate his point. Shaking his finger, he said, "Don't put something too big in your pocket!"

Drawing by Marcel Moyse

PART FIVE – STORIES FROM THE WOODWIND CLASS: 1967 – 1981

THE MUSIC OF SILENCE

AN INSPIRATIONAL WOODWIND CLASS

CHAMBERMUSIC

LIMITS OF PERCEPTION

TEA CEREMONY

MY BIG MISTAKE

"AND NOW, TAKE ME TO PARADISE."

"An inability to stay quiet is one of the conspicuous failings of mankind."

Walter Bogehot

THE MUSIC OF SILENCE

For most summers between 1967 and 1980, I participated in Mr. Moyse's woodwind and flute classes in Brattleboro. Most of the students stayed at the Dalem Chalet, owned by a couple who truly enjoyed woodwind music.

Every morning, the music loving lodge owners cleared their huge dining room for our rehearsals. Through large picture windows, we looked out at a beautiful green meadow with mountains all around. As the lodge was used primarily for skiers in the winter, our woodwind class had the entire place to enjoy, dine in and rehearse in.

Mr. Moyse liked to dine with us after class. Since surgery had removed part of his stomach, he ate very slowly, but heartily. He thoroughly enjoyed his food, never seeming to miss his sense of smell.

After dinner, as the other participants graciously adjourned, he invited me to sit with him; he profoundly enjoyed our silent companionship.

As we sat together, I learned to appreciate the beauty and importance of silence in our lives. I realized that silence can be more musical than music itself. And I came to understand that few people have true silence in their lives, even though silence gives one a profound sense of inner peace.

"Without silence, there is only noise."

Scott Peck

AN INSPIRATIONAL
WOODWIND CLASS (1975)

Fifteen woodwind players (three flutists, three oboists, three clarinetists, three French hornists and three bassoonists) were assembled and tuned up, ready to begin an inspiring class. The French horn player set his chair and music stand in front of Moyse and began with a melody he chose from *Tone Development Through Interpretation.* This was Moyse's published personal collection of 90 melodies from opera, ballet and classical pieces, for the "the study of expression, vibrato, color, suppleness and their application to different styles."

This performer, a seasoned professional with a meltingly delicious tone, was playing *The Flower Aria* from Bizet's *Carmen.* As he ended the excerpt, Moyse inspired him to bring out more expression in his playing. Like Merlin the magician, Le Maitre magically transformed the player through his singing and miming, illustrating the setting, drama and flavor of the aria. When the musician performed the piece a second time, he played at a new level.

* * * * * * * * *

A young protégé from John Mack's oboe studio, played *Meditation from Thais* by Massenet.

As Moyse worked with him on the setting of the piece, carefully balancing the color of the low tones and creating the right atmosphere, the young professional transformed this famous violin solo into a magnificent oboe solo.

* * * * * * * *

A 17-year-old Curtis Institute bassoon student played an aria from Gounod's *Faust.* Moyse said jokingly, "You are too sharp, we need to buy you another." Then, he went on to enlighten the student, bringing out his rich tonal colors; helping him to create a sound that had the depth of an operatic baritone.

* * * * * * * *

These astonishing "students" were already highly accomplished. But Moyse's dramatic explanations of settings and meanings behind plots facilitated musical expression—to sing and to talk on their instruments. As they greatly expanded their range of dynamics, color and nuances, the music they played became more and more vivid! I found it equally thrilling to be a player or a listener.

Mr. Moyse encouraged students to play a melody from his *Tone Development Through Interpretation* to begin a class and sometimes additionally after a break. An appropriate selection became a wonderful spiritual warm-up, enlivening the following performance of a much rehearsed chamber work.

I could write a chapter about any one of these classes. For me, nothing could equal in effect the lasting euphoria I experienced from a day of working with Marcel Moyse.

"It is not what we take up but what we give up that makes us rich."

Henry Ward Beecher

CHAMBERMUSIC

In June, 1973, following a Woodwind Class, I was excitedly telling Mr. Moyse about a year I spent with my musical family in Edinburgh, Scotland.

I described the simplicity of our lives. We had no TV, computers, central heating, refrigerator or clothes dryer. But without these "distractions," our family was deeply enriched. I described our impromptu musicales, accompanied by an old out-of-tune upright piano in the dining room!

I also related stories of weekly invitations to play chamber music with many fine musicians. At these delightful gatherings, we assembled in a horseshoe formation facing an enormous blazing fireplace in an unheated castle-like stone room. A crowd of enthusiastic people huddled around our shoulders. They were simultaneously keeping themselves warm and becoming intimately involved in the music. I recall marveling at the fun and true camaraderie of these occasions, and at how happy I was to be a musician!

Moyse replied, "….Of course! Scotland is a poor country! For me, there were similar gratifying occasions in my poor apartment in Montmartre."

LIMITS OF PERCEPTION

Moyse used humor as his unique method of breaking down students' resistance to learning new concepts. He always had a humorous situation or joke to tell that uncannily related to the music being studied. Like Mulla of Nasrudin, the Middle Eastern Sufi, or Franz Buppi, the German buffoon, he told fables using animals and purposely-foolish human characters or situations. He often slipped in profound concepts sideways, relating ideas that were well beyond ordinary established patterns of thinking.

The less developed students understood his jokes superficially. However, their playing became more relaxed and their tones improved; they had a good time being entertained. Students with deeper perceptions began to understand his humor on more profound levels.

Additionally, it was possible for a student to advance to new and higher levels through the power of his teachings. Enlightenment occurred not only in that person's playing, but in his/her attitude about music and life.

Mr. Moyse's fables were so engaging that students were often inspired to tell him hilarious stories of their own. These tales, often told after class at dinners and banquets, were always a delight to Le Maitre.

TEA CEREMONY (1968-1980 and beyond)

Mr. Moyse loved his teatime—which usually occurred around 5 p.m. during a woodwind class break. He made a real performance out of the preparation of his cup of tea. He loved to hear the gasps of his students as he filled teaspoons to overflowing with sugar and ceremoniously counted, one…two…three…four…five…six…seven…eight."

He held each spoonful up high and watched the sugar cascade down into the cup of hot tea. He never stirred it. What he loved most was the wet remainder of tea-flavored sugar at the bottom of the cup!

Vanilla waffle wafers were his favorite addition.

MY BIG MISTAKE (1973)

On a beautiful June day, between the flute and woodwind classes, I made lunch for Mr. Moyse at his double chalet in West Brattleboro. I substituted as cook for Blanche Moyse, his treasured daughter-in-law who lived there.

Cooking in her kitchen went well; my fresh mushroom soup (his favorite) with its secret spice was just right; the rest of the food was perfect.

I brought lunch to Mr. Moyse, who was sitting in the sun on a large wooden deck, looking out at the mountains.

The finale to the meal was tea, which I had brewed and poured into a warm pot.

The sugar bowl was empty. Anxiously looking around for the sugar, I spotted a row of canisters on the counter top. After filling the sugar bowl, I added a spoon and brought it out to Moyse with the tea.

Of course, there was the usual ritual, "one, two, three, four, five, six, seven, eight" heaping teaspoonfuls. He intently watched each one cascade down into the cup.

Then, he took a sip. WOW!! He spat with great force off the deck
– IT WAS SALT!!!

After the shock, he laughed insatiably and said that he would tell his
flute students at his Master Classes in Matsumoto, Tokyo and Kobe,
Japan the following month (at which 5,000 flutists would be present)
that one of his American students had tried to poison him!

"And now, take me to paradise."

Marcel Moyse

"AND NOW,
TAKE ME TO PARADISE."
Marcel Moyse (1971)

It was a lovely June day at Moyse's home in Brattleboro. Marcel's beloved wife, Mimi, had died a few weeks before. His heart was broken but he continued to teach and write.

The *Mozart Serenade, K.388,* was being played by a woodwind octet.

Moyse paused before the exquisite slow second movement was to be played. The theme begins with a beautiful sweep upward. His eyes sparkled expectantly—as if he was waiting to be transported to heaven on a magnificent musical carpet.

"And now, take me to Paradise," he said.

"But wait, it is not necessaire." He settled back in peace and said, "I was married to a gentle......wise......beautiful......dear woman for 61 years. She made my life heaven. I cannot ask for more."

PART SIX – FOR FLUTISTS ONLY

Additional quotes from flute lessons
and classes by Marcel Moyse

ABOUT FLUTE TONE

What is a beautiful tone? Nobody
knows – that is what you decide.

No matter how sad the music, your tone must have
the supreme inner quality of happiness at its center.

A generous heart creates a beautiful tone.

The tone is a living thing.

The breath is the life of the tone.

The breaths are the vitamins of the tone.

Think how a flower or leaf vibrates with life
sometimes it has an almost imperceptible
shimmer. Think of your tone that way.

The middle "e" on the flute slips   first you have
it, and then phfft – like a wet fish in your hand.

156

Mr. Moyse, I love your tone!
Which one?

Be generous with your tone.

The tones we make are colored — like an artist
uses his palette — to create the atmosphere. A
good flutist does not maintain a single sound,
but varies his tone according to the style,
character, emotion, and composer's language.

How do you get a clear, resonant tone? Listen to
the tap of my pipe against my crystal glass...and
now, with my hand on the glass...it becomes dull.

An important note with a beautiful tone, like the
clear tone of a beautiful bell, will keep sounding
in the ear of the listener, holding that sound until
the next important one comes to replace it. (Listen
to Marcel Moyse recording of the Genin Carnival
of Venice variations for a great example!)

Live inside the music.

Penetrate inside the note.

Focus—Not Force!

Shimmering!

Your lips must always be supple:
they move like little acrobats!

Luminous!

Open – Naturelle! I love the
naturelle...I love astronomy.

ABOUT FLUTE PLAYING

More quotes from Marcel Moyse
flute lessons and classes.

Love the flute, but don't forget the music!

Say with your music, ..."I AM A FLUTIST!!"

Playing the flute is exactly like singing, except
for one thing: the location of your vocal chords.

When you have a problem, create a
small exercise for yourself.

The remedy is within you -
- you must find it yourself.

Sing on your flute!

What we play _is_ the life!

(For your teacher, and for yourself) play it twice
    if the first time was very good, it might
have been an accident – see if you can do that
again – better. If the first time was not good,
you now have the chance to redeem yourself!

My lips, myself, vibrato comes through the
excitation of the phrase. Always changeable.

Misdirected vibrato can give an
impression of instability.

Stimulate your emotional center.

You know, the flute is a weak instrument,
    but we can be a little free   warmer.

Don't try to play too loud, play more generous. It is
not by force, it is in the timing and the love.

Simplicity is elegance.

I don't care where you bought your flute
    Where can I buy your lips?

When we try to sing on our flutes, we are trying to do what comes more naturally to the singer – it is the nearest to the heart.

When I perform, I constantly ask myself, Do they get it?

Don't play the note – sing the note!

Dream the top note.

When you diminish the note, you dream at the same time.

I play flute because I love flute!

I want my money's worth – every note clear.

Do not squeeze the note, make it gorgeous.

Articulation is a kind of language.

Your articulation needs to be <u>clear</u>!

Strong life (in your playing) is not necessarily loud.

Why do you slap that note? Instead, caress the note.

Don't play that way because I told you,
but because now _you_ feel it.

Your wish to be different is not enough.

There is nothing wrong with playing a piece in a
variety of ways – but please do so within the limits,
within the character and structure of the piece itself.

Regarding Baroque music, the melodic line should
shine through the ornaments.

It is not difficult to play fast; it is
difficult to understand and to learn.

It is easier to play fancy and difficult than
it is to make the effort to be a great artist!

Virtuosity can be an expressive art, but it _must_
be in the service of illuminating the work.

You are a musician, you build a structure with
everything in the right place. You play the
chief notes like you build a cathedral, brick
by brick with understanding of the form, the
structure and character of the composition.

When you practice, avoid what is wrong in your
instrument, but instead, make a beautiful
note your teacher, or alternatively, make
that good phrase the teacher for another.

Never play in a sadness way.

Don't make excuses.

If you cannot be an auditor, I cannot
accept you later as a participant.

About practicing: "In a half hour, I change
completely. I am a different man."

I am a good teacher, I practice what I teach.

I am teaching you to teach yourself.

Did you buy your C# in the 5 cent store?

(To a student playing too fast)
Do you have to catch a train?

He plays as if he had weights in his shoes – Heavy.

The flutist plays like a fencer, not a boxer.

Create a shining star!

dolce

...Now, richer!

Caress the note.

Penetrate inside.

Develop, but not by crescendo.

Staccato is <u>not</u> like dried peas
falling down (hard) stairs!

Don't cut my tail!

(About smooth playing): Play without moving with a warm tone. Notes change by surprise, as if someone else is doing the fingering.

Boldness comes from a clear knowledge of the composer's piece, well analyzed and yet spontaneous.

LIFE! LIFE!

GIVE LIFE!

NOW, WAKE THE SLEEPING PEOPLE!

**Note: Moyse did not want to teach "breathing" because he knew that focus on the music created the will on the part of the player to breathe in the right ways. For himself, he sometimes enjoyed the "apologize" breath. He said, "You can breathe anywhere, but your job is to make it sound convincing." (Sometimes, he used the "apologize breath." I leave it to the reader to decipher that meaning.)

PART SEVEN – FOR MUSICIANS

Quotes about making music by Marcel Moyse

If you do not kiss the people with your music, they will never (n-e-v-e-r) kiss (keeeeees) you!

Without the heart, the brain cannot produce music.

Music is the language of love.

Good! Play that again for my pleasure.

You are an actor; you are creating the characters the composer called for. In music, it is important to bring out character not caricature!

The appoggiatura says "Je t'aime" (I LOVE you.)

Open your heart!

That note needs to join the family!

When I perform, I constantly ask
myself, "Do they get it?"

Find the simple way to express the phrase.

Vibrato — Know when to introduce it.
Vibrato comes through the excitation of
the phrase — always changeable.

Caress the note!

I caress one note and give the rhythm with another.

Leave that note with regret.

...needs a special color on the chief note,
and a different color on the others.

A flea has more life than an elephant; he jumps
thousands of times his height — That is staccato!

Analyze the construction of the piece. What is the
form? Analyze this phrase. What are the chief notes?

The music has a life of its own. I
try to let it come through.

You create the atmosphere...already
the forest smells good.

The number three is the magic number in musical
composition — it is not too small and not too big.

The difference between Mozart and Beethoven is that
each would often repeat a phrase three times. On the
third time Beethoven might cry, but Mozart would
become charming. I played 55 performances of the C
Major Flute and Harp Concerto with Lily Laskine.

**"The sonatas of Mozart are unique; they are too
easy for children, and too difficult for artists."**
Artur Schnabel

Mozart is Mozart, even if you play it
bad(ly). Some passages are light, some are
charming, and sometimes the two together!

Every artist was once an amateur. I
prefer the attitude of the amateur.

You are a musician; you build a structure
with everything in the right place.

Every composer deserves the same effort, the
same respect to every detail. I love Mozart
and I also love John Phillip Sousa.

You have to give your best in chambermusic.

It is curious...

Count first; you watch and watch, then jump!

Play with love – everything.

You are a musician; you build a structure
with everything in the right place.

Some music is like a conversation.

I would like something more mysterious (here).

Syncopation is a kind of death or break in life (a break in the natural rhythm) and, In French, syncobe means, "to faint". (Therefore) After the syncopation you must diminish, that is natural. It is not only the syncopation, but also the sentiment (that is necessary).

Make that passage the teacher for the other.

Show you are happy.

Don't cut my tail!

(Remark to French horn player): Play like the tenor sings! You have something to say.

Put some air between....

Don't put something too big in your pocket.

Articulation goes with the form, not with your own facility. It is a kind of language.

Appoggiatura – Why? – The composer put it there because he loved the note.

The appoggiatura is strange – it does not belong to the chord. It needs to be special, and always with expression.

Leave that note with regret!

(To a bassoonist): You are sharp. We need to buy you another. (Laughter.)

Dream the top note.

Show, not by accent, but by feeling.

Caress the note.

.........Now, richer!

Penetrate inside.

In music there are never two measures the same.

Develop, but not by crescendo.

Staccato is <u>not</u> like dried peas falling down stairs!

Give a little warmth – a little sonority here.

Bring out the richness in those low notes. Put your
spoon in and stir the myonaize (mayonnaise).

It is the silence between the notes
that makes the music.

Silence is constantly speaking – it is
necessary for the flow of music.

For myself, <u>most</u> important is rhythm.

Pay the debt!

Count first; you watch and watch, then jump!

Immediately, I should have the tempo. Are you waiting for the tone to be better? (laughter)

If you do not keep the beat, I become sick.

Even with a groppetto, I keep the rhythm, the proportion. Don't put something too big in your pocket!

You can trust the music in a free way—if it makes sense.

Play the last phrase like a souvenir.

NOW, WAKE THE SLEEPING PEOPLE!

CPSIA information can be obtained at www.ICGtesting.com
Printed in the USA
LVOW11*2343200716

497128LV00002B/2/P